EFFECTIVE COLLABORATION

STRATEGIES FOR PURSUING COMMON GOALS

SECOND EDITION

Teresa Hogue and Jeff Miller

ROCKY MOUNTAIN PRESS
a division of the *Rocky Mountain Institute for Leadership Advancement*
524 Emery Street
Longmont, CO 80501
1.888.709.0088
www.rmleadership.com

ORDERING INFORMATION
For individual sales, quantity sales, and orders for college
textbook/course adoption use contact the publisher at the
address listed above.

Printed in the United States of America

ISBN 1-929149-11-5

In the past several years, communities, organizations and businesses have helped bring positive solutions to tough issues. Your issue could be next. Do you have a productive idea that will make your community and/or organization better?

This book and its practical work sheets will help you and others mobilize and produce results. This book helps teams of people with an extraordinary range of services. It helps to guide critical thinking questions such as:

- *Why* invest in collaboration?

- *What* level of commitment and collaboration will serve us best?

- *How* can we best engineer constructive processes for beginning, struggling and growing collaborative efforts?

- *Who* takes action and *when*?

The *goal* of this book is simple:

> *To get individuals and groups in touch with the reality of using community-based collaboration technology*
> - on **time**,
> - with the best **tools**, and
> - *at the right **price***.

The ideas, tools and framework provided have helped local communities and organizations in the United States, Canada, England, and Guam. The technology of collaboration has successfully been used in a wide range of communities of interest facing tough issues related to public safety, health and human services, environmental and natural resources, education, culture and arts, and economic development.

Additionally, the technology has been used to collaborate among and with private and public sectors, organizations who traditionally competed with one another for resources, and for-profit and not-for-profit businesses.

Table of Contents

HOW TO USE THIS BOOK TO MOVE BEYOND THE EXPECTED TO REALITY

Most people and groups want to grow beyond the issues and problems facing them today. Built on this belief, people are embracing leadership supporting the *development* of practical strategies *before* problems emerge. Success and growth — either as a development strategy or for addressing a problem — trigger obvious questions:

How *does a community grow successfully when so many issues are complex and seem overwhelming?*

How *do some communities build close-knit cultures of people and organizations to lead and sustain positive change and why do others fail?*

How *the agility of a local community continued as it becomes a **learning community**, one that works to provide for its future generations?*

How *much collaboration is enough?*

This workbook's first aim is not to let the users become seduced by collaboration and growth. The temptation to increase success and double the numbers of people and groups involved sends a wave of euphoria through the minds of funders, leaders and other decision makers. Usually, this is when efforts begin to identify trouble.

Rather, the aim of this workbook is to offer a blueprint for critical thinking and action. The workbook helps those involved decide if, when and to what degree collaboration will be a positive investment. It moves the users beyond just *having good meetings* to real and practical support for healthy communities and organizations.

The authors draw upon experience, research and education with a wide variety of community-based collaborative efforts. Regardless of the communities or organizations, two characteristics are apparent —

1. During the past decade, individuals and groups do more in a day than entire departments did 10 years ago. Soon, this pace will be elevated as the information age becomes an everyday reality.

2. Successful collaborative efforts don't just happen; they use collaboration technology and core principles supporting servant leadership to make profound change.

Initiating Collaborative Efforts

A new spirit of working together is surfacing all across the country and world. This is occurring in the workplace, in neighborhoods, among friends and in places of worship. Working together successfully occurs in environments where people feel safe and secure coupled with knowing their contribution is valued.[1]

Collaborative working relationships are fostered when people, their interests and their values are closely tied.[2] To create and sustain these environments, people have to be involved in ways that they see success, discuss improvements, and celebrate outcomes.

Generally, two *types* of collaborative working environments exists —

- **Geographic organizations and/or communities** – people and organizations gather as a result of the ***places*** where they live, work, play, and/or call home.

- **Organizations and/or communities of interests** – people and organizations gather as a result of common ***interests*** held with little attention paid to geographic boundaries.

Throughout this book, the working environment plays a significant role in building and sustaining collaborative efforts. The people seated at the table represent the very core of collaboration — **the working environment**.

---

[1]Parker, 1996
[2]Gray, 1989

FOUR *LENS* OF COLLABORATIVE CHANGE —

Throughout this book, four *lens* will be used. Each part helps the user mobilize the complexity of working collaboratively.

Using This Book

Like multiple gears in a well-running engine, working collaboratively depends on multiple parts working in synchronization. Although this book provides detail on the parts or gears of collaboration, the user is expected to tie the information into a system of support for working collaboratively.

The book consists of four parts beyond the introduction. Part One addresses the underlying core principles and elements of working collaboratively. Part Two helps people and organizations identify the rationale and capacity to engage in collaboration. The Six Sections of Part Three describe the framework for building and sustaining the infrastructure of working collaboratively. Finally, Part Four provides practical tools supporting growth, development and ways to measure progress.

Part 1 — Core Principles and Elements

The underlying beliefs and values of working together collaboratively are based on four core principles. These principles are supported by elements and methods that put the principles into operation.

Part 2 — Frames of Reference

Mobilizing and sustaining collaborations rests on common understanding and communication of how people and groups successfully work together. Each part of this book contains information, education and research referred to as **frames of reference**.

Part 3 — Application

Opportunities to apply core principles and frames of references are provided throughout this book. The user is encouraged to work with others and apply efforts to real issues the group faces.

Part 4 — Reality Check

Working together effectively rests on group consensus and conclusions. The Reality Check section found at the end of each part provides a profile for actual courses of action the collaborative effort takes.

Part I — Principles and Elements of Working Collaboratively

During the past decade, individuals and groups often do more in a day than entire departments did ten years ago. Soon, this pace will be elevated as the information age becomes an everyday reality. Successful collaborative efforts don't just happen; they use collaboration technology and core principles. At the very center of the core principles is the belief in **stewardship**.

Center Principle – Stewardship

Beginning with the center principle of stewardship shapes the mind-set of people and groups being accountable for the well-being of the larger group, organization and/or community. As stewards, individuals and collaborations of people and groups operate in an environment of service rather than control. As Peter Block states, *"…it is accountability without control or compliance."*[3]

Two characteristics are evident when stewardship is the core of a collaborative effort:

1) members exhibit the vitality, enthusiasm and spirit needed to elevate excellence, and

2) every member of the collaborative effort experiences a true sense of meaning and purpose.

Core Principles – Community, Servant Leadership, Capacity, Collaboration

In the quest to develop healthy collaborative systems of support, four ***CORE PRINCIPLES support the center principle of stewardship***. The core principles are applied in significant ways in all areas of developing, mobilizing and sustaining collaborations. Each work interdependently of each other and cross the boundaries of work in the for-profit, not-for-profit, public and private sectors.

---

[3]Block, 1998

STEWARDSHIP

Community is the first step in bring together people and organizations who share a purpose. The significance of the work of the community is the joy of doing rather than the goods and services produced. Viewing community with little value is the greatest waste of human potential and social capital.[4]

Servant Leadership is best described as an individual and/or group that chooses service over self-interest. A servant leader elevates accountability and productivity without control or compliance and is a key factor in reducing fragmentation and moving beyond debate.[5] Practicing servant leadership distributes power, purpose and rewards among a diversity of people and groups. Servant leaders are characterized by:

- **Balance of power**:
  People act on their own choices and lead actions tailored to meet needs.

- **Primary commitment**:
  It is to the larger community and does not constrain its attention to individuals or small groups that can breed self-centeredness.

- **Equal and valued participation**:
  Each person defines the purpose and culture of the collaborative effort.

- **Balance and equitable distribution of rewards**:
  All members share in creating its wealth and expanding its resources.

---

[4]Celente, 1997
[5]Spears, 1998

STEWARDSHIP, CONTINUED

Capacity for productive change can and does make the difference between improvement and non-improvement of organizations. Most public and private organizations can be significantly improved at an acceptable cost when a capacity for dealing with transformational change exists.[6] Generally, capacity can be described by establishing and implementing:

- a sense of urgency

- a guiding collaborative effort

- a vision and strategies

- a *change* vision

- broad-based action

- short term wins

- long term gains and growth

- new approaches in the culture

Collaboration is a growing necessity among communities and/ or organizations sharing common interests. In a slow-moving world, organizations need a good executive in charge. In a moderately paced context, teamwork is necessary to deal with the periodic transformations. In a world where information and communication is at a fast pace, teamwork and working collaboratively is enormously helpful almost all the time.[7]

In environments of change, even talented individuals won't have enough time or expertise to absorb rapidly shifting issues and technological information. Individual enterprises won't have the time or ability to communicate decisions to large numbers of people and groups.

---

[6]Kotter, 1996
[7]Useem, 1998

ENGAGEMENT FACTORS — METHODS TO MOBILIZE

The center principle of stewardship and supporting core principles can be mobilized as any collaborative effort begins, develops and becomes sustainable. Engagement factors support:

- discovering new and innovative ways to approach complex issues;
- aid in self-reflection;
- gaining solicitation of opinions, perceptions and ideas;
- support careful listening; and
- remain open to new ideas.

1. Dialogue and Discussion

Dialogue, the exploration of ideas, is critical to developing solutions to the complex issues facing communities today. As communities look toward vitalizing, their health whether economic, environmental, safety, or education the value of a diverse group of people coming together to explore options has contributed to successful efforts tailored to the community.

Discussion follows dialogue as people come to a conclusion or decision about the best actions to take. Without dialogue, the options for discussion are limited and do not support the learning environment of including all human capital.

2. Whole-Systems Approach

Answering the question, *How do we build and sustain more results with more people in more places?* used to mean investing in brand new projects and all that go with them. Today, greater sustained success is found when whole-systems approaches are used in practical and realistic ways.

Whole-systems approaches utilize all systems available to the members of the collaboration with potential for creation, modification, and reinsertion.[8] This approach accomplishes two critical outcomes: It brings maximum experience and wisdom to the table, and in remarkably short time, turns those resources into action. It creates new, aligned systems, goals, roles, procedures, and sustainable result. It accelerates servant leadership, commitment and ownership of change by involving a diversity of people in decisions.

---

[8]Zohar, 1997

ENGAGEMENT FACTORS — METHODS TO MOBILIZE, CONTINUED

3. Force Field Framing and Reframing

Which collaborative efforts are assertive enough to succeed in competitive and complex environments? Those groups that continue to examine the forces working for and against their efforts to succeed. Generally, four force fields serve to influence ongoing work of any collaborative effort:

- **supporting forces** — key leaders advocating support
- **non-supporting forces** — community apathy
- **the past** — *old guard* leadership willing or unwilling to support new efforts
- **emerging trends** — such as 20 percent population growth projected over 10 years

Using force fields helps to frame and reframe strategies to reach the desired result. This process helps individuals and groups build a sense of value, develop capability, strengthen servant leadership and to be understood by a wide cross section of people.

4. Moving from A to B

An old proverb states, *"If you don't know where you are going, any road will get you there."* **Moving from A to B** provides a process to reach agreement on the end result; **A** represents the current situation, issue or problem while **B** represents the desired condition, outcome or result.

Through discussion, reaching a shared understanding of the current situation bridges perception and reality among a diverse group of people. Describing the current situation takes into account the many beliefs and values of the group.

Through dialogue and discussion, establishing **B** not only builds a shared vision of the future, but frames the flexibility needed to implement positive courses of action. This could be compared to flying between Portland, Oregon and Tokyo, Japan. Though a flight plan is filed for the trip, there is an average of 464 adjustments in the flight plan on each flight. As new information, trends, incidents, resources, etc. emerge during the process of reaching **B**, it is critical for collaborative efforts to be flexible enough to **adjust** the flight plan.

Applying Center Principle, Core Principles and Engagement Factors

Center Principle — Stewardship

In a group, use dialogue to address the topics provided. Seek to gain understanding of each person's beliefs and values.

If stewardship is authentic self-expression that creates value, then:

• How authentic are we as stewards?

_____

_____

_____

_____

_____

_____

• How deep and broad is our self-expression?

_____

_____

_____

_____

_____

_____

• How much value could we create as partners?

_____

_____

_____

_____

_____

_____

Center Principle — Stewardship, Continued

Using the element **A→B**, rate the level of stewardship exhibited today and realistically what level will be in existence within three years.

Today

1	5	10
Low		High

In Three Years

1	5	10
Low		High

Using the element of **Force Field Framing and Reframing**, identify which forces strengthen stewardship and which forces working against reaching a high level of stewardship.

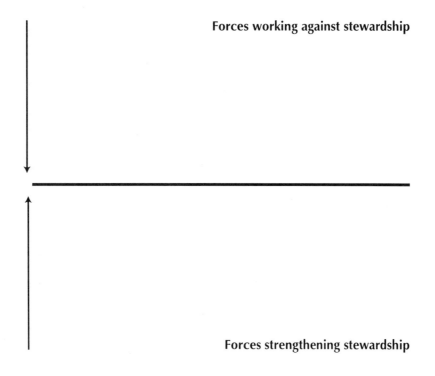

Forces working against stewardship

Forces strengthening stewardship

Core Principle — Community

- Describe the communities, organizations, groups and/or businesses sharing common interest on an issue.

_____

_____

_____

_____

_____

_____

_____

- What brings them to this effort? What will bring them to the effort?

_____

_____

_____

_____

_____

_____

- What forces work against their involvement?

_____

_____

_____

_____

_____

_____

Core Principle — Servant Leadership

Individually, rate the current levels of servant leadership practiced with a dot (•).

Next, use a check (✓) to identify where the group could realistically be in one year.

As a group, compare opinions and hold dialogue and discussions on ways to increase the principle of servant leadership.

1	3	5

High degree of balanced power

High degree of dominance

1	3	5

High degree of commitment to the group and outcomes

High degree of self-centeredness and entitlement

1	3	5

High degree of equal and Valued participation

High degree of a few people making decisions for many

1	3	5

High degree of shared responsibility

High degree of ownership by a few and rewarding people and/or groups

Core Principle — Capacity

Use dialogue to explore existing and potential group capacity. Initiate dialogue using the following questions:

- How urgent is the issue we are concerned about?

_____

_____

_____

- As a group, do we have the skills, knowledge and understanding to build and sustain a collaborative effort?

_____

_____

_____

- Do we have experience and/or the capability to build and execute a vision?

_____

_____

_____

- Among our group, do we have history of engaging a wide cross section of people and groups in something we believe to be important?

_____

_____

_____

- What assets currently exist that we can build upon?

_____

_____

_____

Core Principle — Collaboration

As a group, use the following matrix to explore the potential for working together collaboratively.

The **horizontal axis** calls for identifying *urgent* and *non-urgent* issues, concerns or emerging trends.

The **vertical axis** calls for identifying what is *critical* and what is *not critical*.

This application brings together the four engagement factors —

- dialogue and discussions,
- looking at the whole system of change,
- force field, and
- moving from A → B.

The four quadrants help partners identify all tasks. Those identified in the *Critical – Non-Urgent* quadrant typically become activities of the group providing greatest long term impact.

	Urgent	Non-Urgent
	_____	_____
	_____	_____
	_____	_____
Critical	_____	_____
	_____	_____
	_____	_____
	_____	_____
	_____	_____
Non-Critical	_____	_____
	_____	_____
	_____	_____

REALITY CHECK

Work completed during the application section begins to build a framework for working collaboratively. This section allows the group to apply information and decisions made previously. Complete the **Reality Check** by answering the following questions:

- As a group, we are concerned about: (identify the issue, trend or problem)

_____

_____

_____

_____

_____

_____

- We are willing to be stewards of this concern for the following reasons:

_____

_____

_____

_____

_____

_____

- Our community now consists of: (name the individuals, groups, organizations, cities, etc., involved)

_____

_____

_____

_____

_____

_____

REALITY CHECK, CONTINUED

- This concern will benefit by expanding our community to include: (Name individuals, groups, organizations, cities, etc., you seek to involve.)

  _____

  _____

  _____

  _____

  _____

  _____

- To be successful, we view ourselves as servant leaders. Leadership characteristics that best describe us include:

  _____

  _____

  _____

  _____

  _____

  _____

- Our current capacity to address this issue can be described as:

  _____

  _____

  _____

  _____

  _____

  _____

PART 2 — BEGIN WITH SUSTAINABILITY IN MIND

Part 2 guides exploration of:

- **Paradigm profiles**
- **Roles and responsibilities**
- **Community trends**
- **Capacity profiles**

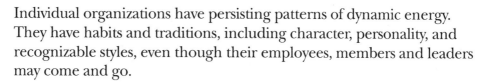

Each plays a critical role in staging the growth, development, implementation and sustainability of working collaboratively.

Working collaboratively stages new paradigms. It builds on a greater pool of potentiality and provides opportunities to interweave patterns of dynamic energy and enthusiasm. When working collaboratively, courses of action manifest deeper underlying resources and accountability.

Individual organizations have persisting patterns of dynamic energy. They have habits and traditions, including character, personality, and recognizable styles, even though their employees, members and leaders may come and go.

Organizations and groups with history don't just happen. They build their successes with *the end in mind*.[9] To exist, they plan first for sustaining their action. They weave their vision, beliefs, or underlying values, in place.

To *ex-ist* in the original Latin literally means *to stand out from*. Existing organizations, groups or communities use their vision to drive success. Their style of leadership and doing business coupled with their basic values inspire their spoken and unspoken code of behavior.

Organizations, groups and communities traditionally focus their efforts on profit, efficiency, success and excellence. New paradigm organizations and collaborative efforts draw their focus on a deeper vision and more lasting values. They see themselves as a part of a larger tradition to include deeper values of stewardship. This may include service to the community, care for the environment and concern for human well-being. They are concerned with sustainability, their own and that of the communities and environment in which they operate.[10]

Bring together organizations, groups, communities and individuals to work collaboratively creates a *new organization, group or community*. Working together successfully rests on exploring common ground and many times, creating common ground.

---

[9]Covey, 1990
[10]Zohar, 1997

PARADIGM PROFILES

Applying Paradigm Profiles, Community Trends, Roles and Responsibilities, and Capacity Profiles

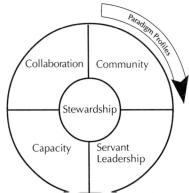

During the next three years, our group will make the greatest impact, shifting from traditional profiles to paradigm profiles.

Completing the Paradigm Profile individually and as a group will frame the mind-set of the group, shape group values, and contribute to the commitment of working together.

There are two profiles listed. The *Traditional Profile* identifies characteristics found in organizations, groups and communities who find it difficult to work collaboratively. The *Paradigm Profile* lists characteristics associated with collaborative efforts that reach and sustain success.

PARADIGM PROFILES, CONTINUED

Using the scale provided, indicate with a dot (•), where the group members fall on a continuum today. With a check (✓), identify where the group can *realistically* be in three years.

Traditional	Profile	Paradigm
Certainty	←————————————→	Uncertainty
Predictability	←————————————→	Rapid Change; Unpredictability
Hierarchy	←————————————→	Nonhierarchical Networks
Division of labor is functionally fragmented	←————————————→	Multifunctional and integrated efforts
Power emanates from top or center	←————————————→	Power emanates from interacting centers
Citizens or staffs are passive about production	←————————————→	Citizens and staffs are co-creative partners
Single viewpoint	←————————————→	Many viewpoints
One best way	←————————————→	Multiple ways
Competition	←————————————→	Cooperation
Inflexible structures	←————————————→	Responsive and flexible structures w/ shared control
Bureaucratic control	←————————————→	Efficient, meaningful service and relationships
Top-down reactive	←————————————→	Bottom-up exploring

Paradigm Profiles, Continued

• Collectively, we agree the paradigms supporting our efforts include:

_____

_____

_____

_____

_____

_____

_____

_____

• Collectively, we agree traditional methods of working together that do not support our efforts include:

_____

_____

_____

_____

_____

_____

_____

_____

COMMUNITY TRENDS

An investment that takes community further...
and you along with it.

Today, group collaboration efforts utilize both traditional and non-traditional methods to solve problems. Whether members use the public library to research solutions or cell phones to communicate from a remote area, capitalizing on all trends and technology can be a critical component of communication, collaboration and success.

Behind each success is a host of people constantly scanning the environment. This fundamental task contributes to planning, implementation and adjustment needed in high performing collaborative efforts.

Needs assessments provide clear definition of problems and potential solutions. However, they provide little if any opportunity for dialogue and discussion about the future. Examining immediate and future changes along with trends provides a platform for proactive solutions.

Eight community trends have been identified.[11] Using the scale provided, *individually* identify where you believe your community is today. As a *group,* compare perceptions and discuss what conditions are working for or against the trends.

Following the completion of action, identify trends and changes observed in the community or organizations such as economic shifts, crime rate or population shifts, and map the current and projected environment.

Example

Small communities rely on:

One economic base   Multiple bases

Conditions working to support this shift include:
- demands for new products
- more highly skilled labor
- more industry growth

Conditions working against this shift are:
- more unskilled people
- *no-growth* value
- limited transportation

Trends emerging in our community today:
- more new people moving into area
- new housing starts
- higher percentage of school-age youth and senior population

[11]McRae, 1994

Community Trends, Continued

Eight community trends

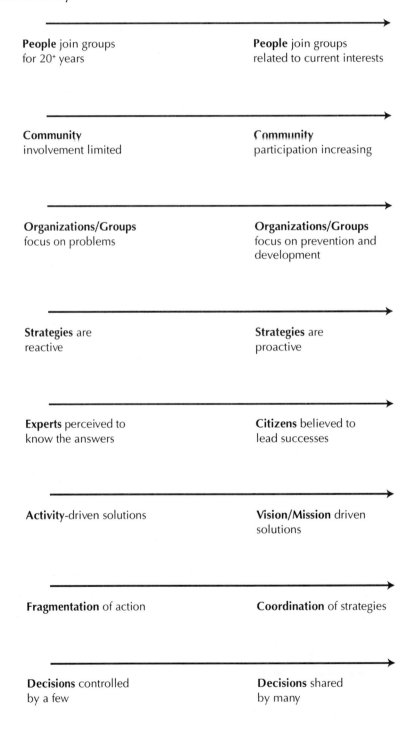

People join groups
for 20⁺ years

People join groups
related to current interests

Community
involvement limited

Community
participation increasing

Organizations/Groups
focus on problems

Organizations/Groups
focus on prevention and
development

Strategies are
reactive

Strategies are
proactive

Experts perceived to
know the answers

Citizens believed to
lead successes

Activity-driven solutions

Vision/Mission driven
solutions

Fragmentation of action

Coordination of strategies

Decisions controlled
by a few

Decisions shared
by many

ROLES AND RESPONSIBILITIES

Peter Senge, author of **The Fifth Discipline** and champion of transformational change says, *"It would take a genuine flight of fantasy to both take seriously the multiple, interdependent challenges involved in sustaining profound change and still hold the view that change happens because great leaders drive change from the top."*

How could one individual or a small group at the top of a hierarchy possibly deal with the range of challenges present?

The principles, paradigms and trends described support Senge's studies. Likewise individuals feel powerless to make a real impact on complex issues.

Building on the center principle of stewardship combined with core principles an engagement factors strengthens organizations, groups and communities to form natural networks of diverse people who share common interests.

Servant leadership is a significant principle as new roles and responsibilities begin to emerge. As dialogue and discussion lead to action, implementation and new or expanded systems of support, people and groups shift from self serving to serving the whole. Servant leaders build and maintain community capacity, *the combined influence of a community's commitment, resources and skills deployed to build community strengths and address existing and future issues.*

Community roles and responsibilities supporting healthy communities is an important step in creating, maintaining, expanding and sustaining collaborative efforts. The capacity of individual and group roles and responsibilities is enhanced through *learning. Learning* through experience, following a track or discipline, and generating knowledge that shapes the collaborative culture.

To begin this learning process, individuals and groups engaging in the **A→B** element will further identify their strengths and weaknesses as servant leaders. The demise of collaborative efforts often rests in unclear expectations, roles and responsibilities, and not because of good intentions by committed people and groups.

Instructions:

Using a force field begins to define the culture of roles and responsibilities serving in the best interests of working collaboratively. Periodically returning to this activity will contribute to refining roles and responsibilities.

(Circle) the words best describing **Current** roles.

Place a check ✔ on the words best describing the **Future**.

Negative Roles

Cynicism	Focus on division	Hold grudges
Not in my backyard!	Solution wars	Polarization
Narrow interests	Frustrations	Hoarding Power
Win-Lose solutions	Mean-spiritedness	Me-first
Politics of personality	Nothing works	Attacking
Surly behavior	Blockers & blamers	Dividers
One line zingers	Re-debate the past	Parochialism

Optimism	Focus on unification	Reconciliation
We're in this together	Solving Problems	Trust
Consensus building	Broad, diverse interest	Patience
Interdependence	Win-win-win solutions	Stewardship
Politics of substance	We can do it!	Listening
Challenge ideas	Problem solvers	Healers
Dialogue & discussion	Focus on the future	Sharing Power

Positive Roles

CAPACITY PROFILES

Examining existing and potential community capacity contributes to developing and sustaining vital collaborative efforts. Seven categories of measure are provided.

As a group, rate the current and potential capacity of the organizations, groups and communities interested and/or involved in collaborating.

Participation

Participation should inlcude a diverse number of individual citizens as well as agencies, organizations, businesses and groups.

High	Medium	Low

When responding, consider the number individuals/groups involved, **and** the diversity of people — does participation truly represent a wide variety of people in the community?

Leadership Base

Community leaders bring new people into decision-making, foster positive experiences, productivity and build leadership skills in the group.

High	Medium	Low

Leaders can be defined as those who **believe in themselves, believe in others and believe in the community**. Discuss who the leaders of the group are. Who really gets things done?[12]

---

[12]McCall, 1993

Capacity Profiles, Continued

High Level of Skills

There are a broad range of people possessing a variety of skills, experience and willingness to participate. There are people willing to gain new skills necessary to support successful outcomes.

High	Medium	Low

When responding, consider a wide range of skills — those who has expertise as visionaries, planners, evaluators, implementers, educators, designers, etc.

Shared Understanding and Vision

There is a wide cross-section of youth and adults who share understanding of the desired future along with the vision and overall direction.

High	Medium	Low

When responding, consider why you believe people share understanding and vision for the community. Is it discussed in formal or informal settings? Are groups discussing their contributions to the vision? Does the media keep it in the open?

CAPACITY PROFILES, CONTINUED

Strategic Community Agenda

Clubs, organizations, agencies and groups consider how they contribute to the future and plan together. Generally, roles and responsibilities are clearly defined and accepted.

High   Medium   Low

Communities today often inform the public in a variety of ways — web sites, media, meeting agendas, community report cards, forums and celebrations.

Consistent, Tangible Progress

Community members and collaborative partners are focused on results and real impacts. As new scenarios develop, they adjust plans and report progress on a regular basis.

High   Medium   Low

While funders generally request reports of accomplishment or progress reports, it is critical to define a **portfolio of progress**. Beyond funding, what are the measures of progress for the people involved? For those who benefit from progress?

Capacity Profiles, Continued

Effective and Efficient Organizations, Agencies and Groups

A wide variety of community groups are run well and effectively, monitor their efficiency and the role they contribute to the community.

High   Medium   Low

Consider characteristics of effectiveness and efficiency, such as quality leadership, management and administration, services and support provided, resources used and given, the organizational structure and communication.

Complete the following questions:

• Collectively, our greatest capacity assets include:

_____

_____

_____

• Collectively, our liabilities include:

_____

_____

_____

• Collectively, our aim is to increase our capacity to:

_____

_____

_____

REALITY CHECK

Information applied in Part 1 begins to build a framework for working collaboratively.

Part 2 introduces the reality of building in sustainability – even before defining the specifics of any collaborative effort. This step strengthens the framework by developing the environment and culture in which the collaboration can and will succeed.

Part 2 **Reality Check** captures the beliefs and values of people and organizations. It helps define the **change potential** and the *capacity, confidence and adaptability* to lead collaborative efforts.

Our Capacity to Sustain a Collaborative Effort Includes:

Our recognition that our assets or strengths to build and sustain our collaborative effort can be described in the following profile:

Paradigms

- Our openness to work in new paradigms is described as:

_____

_____

_____

_____

_____

Trends

- The trends in our community, organizations and among our people supporting our collaborative effort are described as:

_____

_____

_____

_____

_____

REALITY CHECK, CONTINUED

Capacity

- Realistically, our capacity to undertake building and sustaining a collaborative effort is best described as:

High: _____

_____

_____

_____

_____

Low: _____

_____

_____

_____

_____

- Productive characteristics members contribute to our collaboration can best be described as:

_____

_____

_____

_____

_____

_____

PART 3 — COLLABORATION TAKING RESULTS FURTHER

In Part 1 and 2 you and others have framed the center core of a collaborative effort.

Part 3:

- **Clarifies and defines** collaborations
- **Tracks** results
- **Builds** strong foundations of support
- **Strengthens** the capacity to operate effectively

The jet engine, like the telephone and antibiotics, is one of those wonders of modern technology that works so well that is has rendered it self mundane. This is the goal of the technology supporting collaboration. That a group of people sharing a common interest can decide to make something positive happen is truly miraculous.

The best result isn't necessarily an object, space or structure – *it's the process.* The process works for everyone involved. Configuring and reconfiguring solutions by choosing from a range of options allow results to be dynamic and adaptable. Functional results tailored to the organizations, groups and communities involved provide a foundation to take results further.

Manufactured results, on the other hand, often miss the mark. Projects are configured and carried out according to particular specifications that are usually meaningless to those they are intended to help. As a result, communities investing in what appears to be easy answers usually end up unhappy.

Collaboration Taking Results Further, Continued

Needs are always changing. The more success is identified, the more needs change around it.[13] Changes will continue to tax the collective abilities of communities, groups and people to deal with them. Therefore, the processes engaging people in reaching real and meaningful result is **value added** by building capacity to address change.

Part 3 introduces six technologies or gears which mobilize collaborative efforts. As in a fine running engine, all six gears are critical to the operations of the collaboration. Missing a gear or a cog on the gear hampers the collaborative work.

Each of the six gears works interdependently with one another. Each gear's effectiveness is impacted by the Center principle, Core Principles, Elements, and the working environments previously described.

As collaborative efforts develop, the gears provide the frames to build and strengthen efforts. On a regular basis, they also provide an avenue to evaluate or monitor efforts. A summary of the six gears is provided. Each gear is defined in detail in each of the following six sections of Part 3.

Information is power.
Diversity is strength.
Complacency is death.
Robert Shaw

---

[13]Normand, 1998

COLLABORATION TAKING RESULTS FURTHER, CONTINUED

1. Linkage

Linkage frames five levels of working collaborative. No two collaborative efforts are the same.

2. People & Group Matrix

Mapping the community, its people, groups; organizations matched with roles and responsibilities.

3. Foundation

Declaring the vision, mission and principles supporting the collaborative effort.

4. Results

Reaching common understanding on the end results.

5. Community Environment

Investing community cultures, traditions, habits and trends in the process of collaborating.

6. Processes and Systems

Exploring strategic processes in creating collaborative systems of support.

1. LINKAGE

Investing in Linking Collaboration

Today's chaotic, turbulent and complex issues support the notion of working together. The system of working together is critical to progressing toward the vision; however, piecemeal approaches rarely if ever prove to be effective.

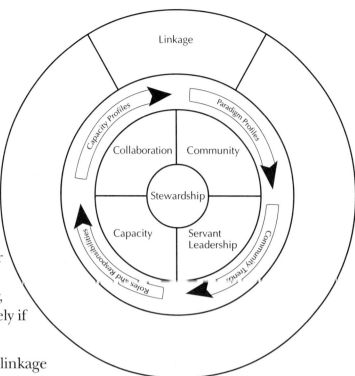

Five levels of collaborative linkage offer define methods to include people systematically. This contributes to the change process and builds capacity for handling the transformation. Selecting and implementing the collaborative level serving in the best interest of the group may push some beyond their comfort zone. This discomfort may be experienced by leaders who traditionally control decisions and by those who have never been involved in real decision making.

Collaborative linkage can help relieve some of this discomfort as it begins to clarify the expectations, roles and responsibilities of those involved. Using this technology can reduce risk and simultaneously increase productivity.

Collaborative linkage occurs in five graduating levels of complexity. The levels range from low or no-risk relationships to interdependent relationships. The levels are designed to work to *support* the collaborative effort. The goal is not to reach the highest level of collaboration, rather to determine the level that best supports the capacity of existing people, groups and resources. The five levels are:

- **Networking**   *sharing* information
- **Cooperation** or **Alliance**   *sharing* activities
- **Coordination** or **Partnership**   *sharing* resources
- **Coalition**   *sharing* systems of support
- **Collaboration**   **creating** new systems

*If we don't change our Direction.
We're likely to end up,
Where we're headed.*

Chinese proverb

COLLABORATIVE LINKAGE (HOGUE, 1994)

LEVEL	PURPOSE	STRUCTURE	PROCESS
Network	• Discussion w/ common understanding • Clearinghouse for information • Create a base of mutual support	• Loose/flexible linkage • Roles loosely defined • Community action link members • Informal communication	• Low key leadership • Minimal decision making • Little conflict
Cooperation or Alliance	• Coordination of matched needs • Limited duplication of services • Group ensures tasks are done • Roles somewhat defined	• Hub serves as central group • Semi-Formal linkages • Formal communication • Group raises money	• Facilitated leadership • Complex decisions • Some conflict • Links are advisory
Coordination or Partnership	• Resources shared for common issues • Resource base creates new resources • New base of support	• Hub includes decision makers • Roles and linkage formalize • New resources developed and joint budget created	• Autonomous leadership • Decision making in hubs and subgroups • Frequent/clear communication
Coalition	• Dialogue and discussion common • Resources realigned from systems • Commitment made for a minimum of three years	• Members engaged in decisions • Roles, time commitment defined • Written linkage agreements • Joint budgets developed	• Shared leadership • Formal decision making • Communication is common and prioritized
Collaboration	• Group accomplishes shared vision, mission, results and impacts • Inter-dependant systems of ongoing support	• Consensus used in decision making • Formal roles, commitment/ evaluation • Linkage is formal and written in work plans and/or assignments	• Leadership, trust and productivity level high • Ideas and decisions equally shared • Highly developed and productive communication patterns

Applying Linkage

Selecting the linkage most appropriate for a collaborative effort is perhaps the most critical communication and commitment pattern established.

Begin by discussing each linkage. Engage force field discussion and identify strengths and weakness contributing to your collaborative efforts.

Don't fall into the trap of assuming the group should aspire to reach a full-fledge collaboration. **Rather**, invest in the linkage serving as the best support for your efforts.

Use the questions provided to guide dialogue and discussion.

- **Currently**, our group is operating in the following linkage:

_____

_____

_____

_____

_____

_____

_____

_____

- We **seek** to move, develop, and/or advance our linkage to:

_____

_____

_____

_____

_____

_____

_____

_____

Applying Linkage, Continued

- The **rationale** for this decision includes:

_____

_____

_____

_____

_____

_____

_____

- The **purpose** of our linkage is to:

_____

_____

_____

_____

_____

_____

_____

- The **processes** important to our success include:

_____

_____

_____

_____

_____

_____

_____

2. People and Group Matrix

Pathways to Diversifying People and Organizations

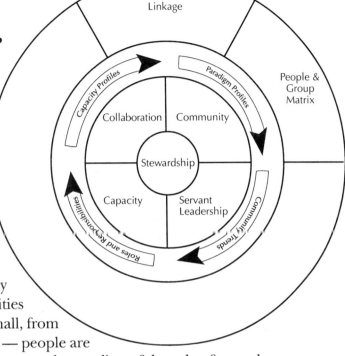

Working collaboratively is an invitation to sidestep the negative messages hitting people about the problems and issues facing society. Across virtually every dimension of our communities — from workplaces to city hall, from classrooms to youth groups — people are giving shape to a profound new understanding of the role of everyday people in solving public problems and issues. Many are breaking free of old assumptions of holding leaders responsible to discover democracy as a rewarding practice, one central to our happiness and effectiveness.

We can't take all the credit for our success, was the headline on the front page of statewide newspaper after a community increased the number of youth completing high school by 32% in three years. This change was lead by a wide cross section of diverse people who view themselves first as servants to others and to the community. They were willing to take risks, provide the vision and structure and, in doing so, showed the way.

People who see themselves as servants first become leaders because they need to become a whole person. In the foreseeable future, servant leaders use the power of persuasion and example as a means to create opportunity and alternatives to build autonomy. Other leaders may use coercive power to dominate and manipulate people resulting in predetermined solutions that destroy autonomy, stifle growth and strengthen resistance to change.

Mobilizing a diversity of individuals, organizations, groups and communities to work together can be complex, and to some, impossible. Implementing a **People and Group Matrix** is a valuable investment in:

- **Clarifying**   - **Identifying**   - **Defining**
- **Framing**   - **Targeting**

2. PEOPLE AND GROUP MATRIX, CONTINUED

- **Clarifying**   **the environment** in which the collaborative effort thrives
- **Identifying** **the interests and culture** of the community
- **Defining**   **expectations, roles and responsibilities** of those involved
- **Framing**   **the people and groups** who may not ***buy-into*** the collaborative
- **Targeting**   **indigenous servant leaders** who have a reputation for engaging others along with providing respected leadership

Building a People and Group Matrix

The success of using the **People and Group Matrix** is not the *number of people and organizations involved*, rather it is developing a *productive mix* to advance collaborative efforts.

Building a **People and Group Matrix** is based on six assumptions:

1. **Diversity**

   Diversity of people and groups adds value to the process and the results.

2. **Commitment**

   Commitment is elevated when people believe they are making a real contribution to something important to them personally and/or professionally.

3. **Expectations**

   Expectations are understood by all involved.

4. **Balancing**

   Balancing the vision, development, action and reflection with people skilled in each task is a sound investment.

5. **Capacity**

   Capacity levels of people individually and collectively will be strengthened in a healthy organization.

6. **Exclusivity**

   Exclusivity builds ideas into action, innovation into infrastructure and capacities into systems.

Building a **People and Group Matrix** is ongoing. It begins with a few people/groups roughly defining the direction of the collaborative effort and its purpose. Re-invention, refinement, and validation continue to evolve as more people and groups become engaged.

Building a People and Group Matrix, Continued

Organization/ Community Pockets Places where people gather		Organization/Community Characteristic Profiles of People				
		Ages of People	Ethnicity	Neighbor-hoods	Leadership Styles	Economic Levels
Recreation Groups						
Faith Groups						
Citizen Groups						
Public Sector						
Private Sector						

Success is not gathering *numbers* of people, but rather, gathering *the right* people for *the right* leadership at the *right time*. In most cases, a small group of people, often called a hub begins the collaborative effort. These are people who are often described as **leaders who get things done.** Their characteristics are described as visionary, action-oriented, thoughtful and professional. They are people who believe it is more important to ask the right questions than provide all the answers.

As the hub builds a **People and Group Matrix**, it first defines **Characteristics** – *the people, age groups, ethnicity, means of income, traditions, and so forth.*

Second, the hub defines **Pockets** – *the wide range of public, private and citizen-based groups, organizations, businesses and agencies within the community.* **Pockets** may also be refereed to as *the places where people gather.*

Applying the People and Group Matrix

Begin by using dialogue to explore characteristics. Ask the question, *How would we describe our organizations and/or community people in real words?*

Second, use dialogue to explore the places people gather to work, play, contribute, participate and mix with others.

Third, use discussion as a means to categorize characteristics and pockets. These should be general descriptions to which specific names of people can be added.

Fourth, use discussion to identify specific *characteristic and pocket profiles.*

Finally, use dialogue and discussion to identify specific people who fit the profiles.

- **Begin**, by generally describing the people, community and organizations – their characteristics:

  _____

  _____

  _____

  _____

  _____

  _____

- **Second**, identify the places – pockets – people gather.

  _____

  _____

  _____

  _____

  _____

  _____

Applying the People and Group Matrix, Continued

• **Third**, identify categories for:

Characteristics	Pockets
_____	_____
_____	_____
_____	_____
_____	_____
_____	_____
_____	_____
_____	_____
_____	_____
_____	_____
_____	_____

(Hint – for convenience, use *sticky notes* to compile each persons input.)

Applying the People and Group Matrix, Continued

The Matrix will be built over time. Initially, the heading for characteristics and pockets may appear like the example below.

Organization/Community Characteristic								
Profiles of People								
Ages of People		Ethnicity		Neighbor-hoods		Leadership Styles		Economic Levels
30% are 55+ years old	40% are 18–54 years old	20% are Native American	29% Hispanic	City View	East Side		New emerging leaders	Under $20,000
								$20,000 to $50,000
30% are 18 and under		40% Anglo	3% Asian	Eagle Springs	Down-town	Strategists	People who mobilize	$50,000 to $90,000
							Peace Makers	$50,000 to $90,000+

Organization/Community Pockets									
Places where people gather									
Recreation Groups		Faith Groups		Citizen Groups		Public Sectors		Private Sectors	
Soccer Clubs	Card Clubs	Catholic	Lutheran	Lion Club	Legion of Foreign Wars	Child Service	Public Schools	Medical	Private School
Gym/Work-out Centers	Running Clubs	Jewish	New Hope	Elks Club	Youth Groups	Forest Service	City Govt.	Legal	Retail
						Elected Leaders	Public Safety	Non-Profit	

Applying the People and Group Matrix, Continued

The next step in developing the matrix is to add individual names of people in the cells. Initially, more than one name often appears in each cell.

Characteristic – Groups

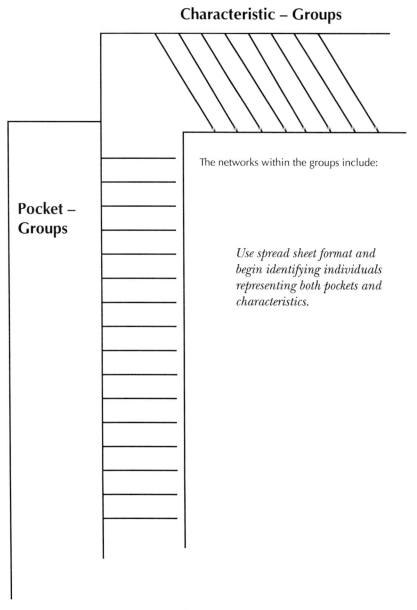

The networks within the groups include:

Use spread sheet format and begin identifying individuals representing both pockets and characteristics.

Pocket – Groups

3. FOUNDATION

IS YOUR COLLABORATIVE EFFORT THE MEANS OR THE END?

Both. Regardless of the level of collaboration, it is the means to deliver results. It provides the diversity of versatility to address complex issues and demands.

Collaboration is the end. It is a system that can be open, flexible and adaptable. It operates with blurred boundaries as it focuses on results. It has the capability to harness fragmented resources within an environment of new or revised platforms and protocols.

Collaboration is the means. Nothing can grow in a self-sustaining way unless there are reinforcing processes underlying its growth.[14] Establishing reinforcing processes begins with building the foundation.

Foundations supporting collaborative efforts are unique. They involve a diverse network of committed people and groups with shared beliefs. Collaborations often bring together those who previously were viewed as competitors. Investing in establishing a foundation provides —

- *Common Ground*

  Opportunities to reach common ground and shared beliefs.

- *Capacity to Advance*

  The safety to advance a ***project*** to ***building a system of growth***.

- *Recognition of Resources*

  Aligning, realigning and leveraging resources toward results first, and ownership second.

---

[14]Senge, 1999

IS YOUR COLLABORATIVE EFFORT THE MEANS OR THE END?, CONTINUED

The foundation of collaborative efforts include three elements:

1. Vision

A vision represents *what is desired* – the underlying condition. A vision is not a service, a product or an event, but the results. A vision is a broad statement created and owned by a wide cross section of people and groups. It is created and sustained through dialogue and discussion. Shared visions are created not by a single committee, but rather by a community.

> *Example:*   *Our community is dedicated to the creation and demonstration of personal, family, business, and community prosperity.*

2. Mission

Mission statements articulate goals, dreams, behaviors, culture and strategies of organizations more than any other document. They clarify *how* a particular group contributes to the vision.

A recent study of change tools such as surveys, rewards, total quality management efforts and reengineering, showed that managers and leaders used mission statements more than any other tool.[15] Mission statements help groups through trying times and in making tough decisions. Successful groups recognize they do not need long discussions about how to handle situations, because the mission statement quickly told them how to act.[16]

Mission statements are not simply mottoes or slogans, but a road map for the group and communities outside the group. Successful groups using mission statements pass three tests. The group owns, articulates and activates the mission.

- *Owns*

  The group believes in their mission and integrates it into everyday work.

- *Articulates*

  The statement is well-written, well-focused, and compelling.

- *Activates*

  Groups members live up to the statement.

---

[15]Jones and Kahaner, 1995
[16]Jones and Kahaner, 1995

©2002 • EFFECTIVE COLLABORATION

IS YOUR COLLABORATIVE EFFORT THE MEANS OR THE END?, CONTINUED

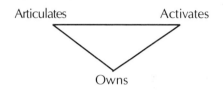

Articulates   Activates

Owns

The Campbell City Alliance

Example: *Community wide, we lead and coordinate planning and review processes that help our citizens build, improve and enjoy their city. Together, Alliance members provide extraordinary service to the neighborhoods in Campbell City, produce decision making processes for growth and development, and measures outcome.*

The Alliance is a role model for citizens, private and public businesses, and elected officials to set the standard for stewardship of Campbell City. It is a model of outstanding cooperation, trust, and communication.

3. Principles

Principles are the operational, ethical and financial guiding lights of the group. Principles are what define group members' beliefs about themselves. In combination with the vision and mission, principles shape goals, dreams, behavior, culture and strategies.

Example: ***The Campbell City Alliance believes in the importance of…***

- ***Success through excellence*** *— Our commitment to excellence drives our efforts to prepare for the future, plan for tomorrow and work today.*

- ***Leadership*** *— As community stewards, we serve our community, its people and their investment in quality of life.*

- ***Growth*** *— We are committed to community-wide growth and achievement for all. We recognize the interdependency of all community resources.*

APPLYING THE FOUNDATION

Establishing the foundation — *the vision, mission and principles – forms a **bull's eye, not a target**.*[17] Any collaborative effort brings together people and groups with: a **History** of policy, practices, procedures within each own organization, and established **Accountability** measures for existing funders and other decision makers unique to their own organization.

Applying the Foundation rests on four elements:

1. Leadership

Leaders are characterized by *believing in **themselves, others** and the **community*** to drive effective collaborative efforts. Leaders interested in reaching the vision with real and meaningful results expand personal effectiveness and add value.

2. Trust

Across the country, there is virtual agreement that talented people determine the success or the failure of any enterprise. The process of identifying, recruiting, engaging, retaining and developing talented people and groups is the critical test. The faster the enterprise grows, the faster it needs to support talented individuals.

Successful collaborations are harnessing the power of trust as a means to build their capacity, aligning the right people for the right job. Focus groups outnumber committees, decision hubs replace executive committees, and work teams support specialized solutions.

3. Commitment

Like competition, collaborative efforts are always a moving target. Collaborations often arise as complex issues become more common. The key for building commitment is to realistically address complex issues and not focus on only simple solutions. Commitment is strengthened by keeping the process moving and focusing on cutting-edge strategies. Today, time is a cutting edge factor and is considered a strategic weapon equivalent to money, productivity, quality and innovation.[18] Commitment can be considered the fuel and the by-product of implementing a vital foundation.

4. Flexibility

Collaboration speeds up information. Ultimately, successful collaborators must be able to tell the difference between creating valuable information and just creating information. The flexible collaborative effort speeds up a communities ability to address if an issue is going to out perform single operations, create new standards and reach visions.

---

[17]Jones and Kahaner, 1995
[18]Webber, 1994

©2002 • EFFECTIVE COLLABORATION

Applying the Foundation, Continued

Using dialogue and discussion, review the four elements.

- **First**, reach agreement on the current value of each.

    Leadership: _____

    _____

    Trust: _____

    _____

    Commitment: _____

    _____

    Flexibility: _____

    _____

- **Second**, identify how the group will strengthen these elements as the collaborative effort grows:

    Leadership: _____

    _____

    Trust: _____

    _____

    Commitment: _____

    _____

    Flexibility: _____

- Our strengths include:

    _____

    _____

    _____

    _____

    _____

Applying the Foundation, Continued

- Soon, our weaknesses will be strengthened by:

_____

_____

_____

_____

_____

- **Third**, begin to shape the vision – *the broad-based desired condition*. Ask each person to complete the following editorial in a state-wide newspaper… ***Someday, our community/organizations will accomplish…***

_____

_____

_____

_____

_____

_____

It is critical each person completes this task independently. Upon completion, ask people to work in groups of three to five people and develop one editorial. This process provides opinions, views and ideas from each person. Ask each group to identify the conditions, lifestyles and/or habits that frames the vision.

- Our Vision Includes

_____

_____

_____

_____

_____

Applying the Foundation, Continued

- **Fourth**, from the editorials, identify the services, tasks, audiences and activities contributing to the vision. These thoughts, ideas and plans from the mission, *the purpose of the collaborative effort*.

Our Mission Includes:

What we do

_____

_____

_____

Who we do it for and with

_____

_____

_____

Our purpose, (why this collaborative effort is necessary)

_____

_____

_____

- **Fifth**, review each group editorial. Identify key words and phrases representing the principles and beliefs group members believe to be important. List the principles important to the group.

_____

_____

_____

_____

_____

_____

_____

_____

_____

Applying the Foundation, Continued

- **Sixth**, refine the work of the group. Concentrate on the content by answering the following questions.

    - What are the top issues the collaboration will address?
      What are the top issues each member organization currently addresses?
      Identify the common ground.

      _____

      _____

      _____

    - What is the most desirable feature of this collaboration?
      What are the current best features of each member organization?
      Identify the common ground.

      _____

      _____

      _____

    - What does the collaboration provide for each member organization?
      What does the collaboration enable our organization to do differently?
      Identify the common ground.

      _____

      _____

      _____

    - What does the collaboration offer the community that does not now exist?

      _____

      _____

      _____

    - Looking ahead, what new opportunities will the collaboration provide?

      _____

      _____

      _____

4. RESULTS

Just Being a Collaboration Won't Guarantee Results.

Collaborative efforts start where individual efforts stop. When conventional efforts become unavailable or are capable of addressing needs and vision, collaborative efforts begin. Collaborative efforts can optimize individual efforts. Working together can advance the vision and clarify desired results and objectives.

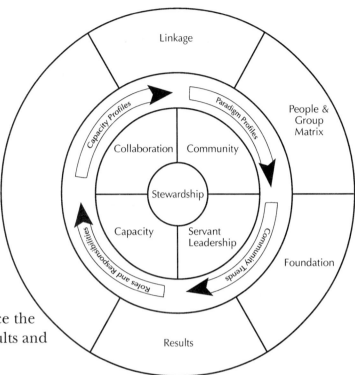

In turn, working collaboratively — *regardless of the level* — provides opportunities to enhance the value of each member in the community, improve assets, provide wider innovation and involvement, and add structure to conventional resources.

Highly effective collaborative efforts share three characteristics:

- **Share** ownership in common vision,
- **Buy into** the mission of the collaborative effort as a process to, and
- **Achieve** results that make a real and meaningful impact.[19]

Collaborations often break new ground. They are capable of addressing issues viewed by individual members as barriers in a new and developing environment.

As the collaborations break new ground, they begin with a vision and mission. Shaping a vision and mission frames the dialogue and discussion that ultimately identifies results or outcomes.

This process clarifies communication and understanding among collaborative members, the people and groups they serve and the broader community. Root causes of less successful collaborative efforts are often found in *muddled results.*[20]

[19]Kuczmarski, 1996
[20]Lofquist, 1983

4. Results, Continued

Successfully shaping results or outcomes is based in three underlying beliefs:

- **Information** is power
- **Diversity** is strength
- **Complacency** is death

These beliefs are repeated endlessly and yet seem somewhat abstract. *Acknowledging* these beliefs is the first step in integrating them as workhorses. *Activating* them in operating a collaboration follows.

APPLYING RESULTS

Begin, addressing results by using the *lens* each person and organization brings to the collaborative effort. Lenses provide opportunities to bring together:

- Assumptions
- Information
- Perceptions
- Reality
- Research
- Complacency

Each is critical in reaching common understanding. With *lens* approach, there is no right or wrong solution, rather reaction, meaning, interpretation, and relevance. *Lenses* help diverse groups of people and organizations move from:

Assumptions to information; activities to systems; and complacency to action.

- Each collaborative member completes the following statements. **In my opinion**... the best result(s) our collaborative effort can achieve is/are:

_____

_____

_____

_____

_____

_____

- With no limits, it is possible for our collaborative effort to accomplish...

_____

_____

_____

_____

_____

_____

RELATIONSHIPS

Everything accomplished in communities is a co-created process, beginning and sustained by vision. It involves people relating to people, organizations relating to organizations and communities relating to communities.

Effectiveness is based on the choices made from moment to moment — how issues are approached, actions are supported and people, organizations and communities respond to one another. Generally, as choices are made, the intention is to *protect* or to *learn*.

Building productive and positive relationships begins with the intention to *learn*, aspiring to do what is *wanted* rather than what is not wanted. A learning environment is sustained when its individuals balance an understanding of:

- Themselves — intra-personal
- Others — interpersonal
- Communities — group

Each member realizes collaborations are not separate entities, they are the collective sum of each member's effort. The collaboration doesn't make decisions, the people involved do. As people contribute to decisions, they actively ask themselves…

- What am *I* contributing to this collaboration?

_____

_____

_____

_____

_____

_____

RELATIONSHIPS, CONTINUED

• And what could I choose differently?

_____

_____

_____

_____

_____

_____

• Do *I* behave in ways that foster learning?

_____

_____

_____

_____

_____

_____

• And what could *I* choose to do differently?

_____

_____

_____

_____

_____

_____

SHIFTING ASSUMPTION TO INFORMATION

The diversity of ideas and opinions identified underscores the importance of addressing complex issues with complex solutions. This is the formula for reaching results and creating some chaos.

Valuing chaos as a resource is an investment in identifying the desired results. Begin by charting broad groups of people who benefit from the vision.

Example:

- **The Vision** *is to support a safe and secure community for children and families.*

- **The Mission** *of the collaboration is to treat abused children and their families and advocate policies, practices and procedures that prevent the abuse of children.*

- **Those who benefit** *include the community, those who are in or have been in abusive environments, those who behave in ways that often lead to abuse, and the network of private and public support systems.*

- **The Community** — *safer community, less crime, lower taxes, behavior changes.*

- **Abused Children/Families** — *treatment services, better parenting, safe places to live.*

- **Those Prone to Abuse or Who Are Being Abused** — *reduced anger, support for change, emotional health.*

- **Private and Public Support Services** — *continuum of timely services, better use of limited resources, family and individual treatment.*

This process shapes *systems of support* rather than individual activities, services or actions. Identifying the people impacted by reaching the vision and how they will be impacted initiates methods to sustain efforts making a real and meaningful impact on the vision.

Shifting Activities to Systems

- Using the information gather in the previous activity, identify the broad categories of those who will benefit.

_____

_____

_____

_____

_____

_____

_____

_____

_____

_____

_____

_____

- Next, identify the benefits for each. Value is added to this process by the diversity of people, ideas, view, opinions and resources.

_____

_____

_____

_____

_____

_____

_____

_____

_____

_____

_____

_____

SHIFTING COMPLACENCY TO ACTION

Action drives progressive collaborative efforts, not complacency. As members of a collaborative effort gain momentum toward action, member organizations will notice impact within their internal operations. Four common characteristics are found among emerging collaborative efforts, and at some point, within member organizations.

1. Real People Impacts

How are people, individuals and groups, impacted? What behavior changes will be identified? What statistics will be changed?

_____

_____

_____

2. Policies, Practices and Procedures

How will the norms of the community change? What policies will be reviewed, changed, or developed in organizations and in the community? What procedures will be different?

_____

_____

_____

3. System Capacity

How can the community be enhanced? What leadership is enhanced or developed? How has a broader base of support been engaged? How are more people and groups engaged?

_____

_____

_____

4. Resource Development

What resources are leveraged? How is the effectiveness and efficiency of existing resources enhanced?

_____

_____

_____

5. COMMUNITY AND ORGANIZATIONAL ENVIRONMENTS

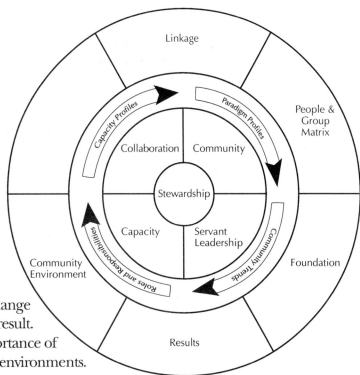

Working Effectively

Ralph Waldo Emerson's said, *"What lies behind us and what lies before us are tiny compared to what lies within us."*

Strengthening community relationships is actually a way of mitigating risks involved with change and opening opportunities for result. This belief gives rise to the importance of community and organizational environments.

"Things are not what they used to be" is heard often. Building successful strategies for complex issues drives people and groups to develop new measures of success and methods of communication, processes and techniques.

However, as new and innovative strategies are implemented, servant leaders recognize the value and importance of merging existing organizational and community environments with their planning. Recognizing the importance of the environment is critical for two reasons:

5-10% those who must innovate, create and lead

85% those who, if properly led, will change

5% the few who never change

1. Generally, most people and groups resist change.

People and groups work with greater efficiency when **habits and traditions** are in place. In this environment, they know what is expected, are acknowledged for their contribution, share in rewards and have a common and understood language. Shifting an environment where habits and traditions are systematic can be disruptive for those uncomfortable with the unknown.

2. Eighty-five percent of the population will thrive in change, if properly led.[21]

Individuals and organizations are not all the same. Some thrive with uncertainty and ambiguity and others have little if any threshold for chaos. Successful leaders get the best out of both, and at the same time, poise themselves to understand the needs, thinking and contributions of the environment in which people work, play and live. Successful strategies depend upon keeping habits and traditions and the environment in balance.[22]

---

[21]Zohar, 1997
[22]Moorthy, 1998

Collaborative Efforts, Regardless of the Linkage, Build New Systems and Neighborhoods

Each collaborative linkage provides opportunities for new or expanded working relationships, communication patterns and responsibility to contribute to a shared vision. Successful collaborative efforts continue to assess the environment. Failure to do so has been demonstrated in lost of time, leadership, money, energy, commitment and results.[23]

Each linkage must be adaptable and responsive to the changing conditions within its environment while preserving overall cohesion and unity of purpose. The leadership must balance a framework for dialogue and discussion, identify what exists today and what is desired in the future (**A→B**), examine strengths and weaknesses (force field), and build an integrated whole system among equals.

The investment of investigating and knowing the environment increases as groups and organizations move from a network linkage to more complex collaborative relationships.

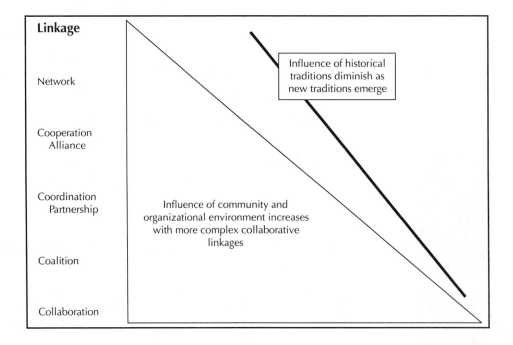

---

[23]Wilcox, 1997

COMMUNITY AND ORGANIZATIONAL ENVIRONMENTAL FACTORS

Investigating and knowing about the environment can be accomplished in a variety of ways. Developing, expanding and sustaining collaborative efforts begins with asking questions, rather than identifying the answers, discover a wider range of information and understanding. Six **Environmental Factors** are common for most organizational and community environments.

1. **Catalysts**

   The events, incidents, or actions bringing issues to the forefront.

2. **History of Working Together**

   The methods, traditions, styles and ways people and groups work together; the culture of how work gets done.

3. **Connectedness**

   The level of interdependent communication, work and connecting achieved.

4. **Political Climate**

   How power and control is exercised and valued; the level of citizen participation.

5. **Policies and Laws**

   Which policies, laws, and/or regulations support/do not support community vitality.

6. **Resources**

   The skills, talents, energy, capitol, assets, etc. supporting the community.

SPIDER WEB

The spider web is a practical tool for learning about community and organizational environmental factors because it is a constructive way to gain input from large numbers of people. Using each person's lens, information can be gathered on:

- **Dialogue and Discussion**

  The strength and weakness of each factor as it relates to the operation of the collaborative effort.

- **Whole Systems Approach**

  Gaining a wide cross section of input and understanding about the issue and ways working collaboratively can be effective.

- **A→B**

  Reaching consensus on the environmental influences – both positive and negative – and desired environments.

Begin, building the **Spider Web** by defining common understanding of each factor.

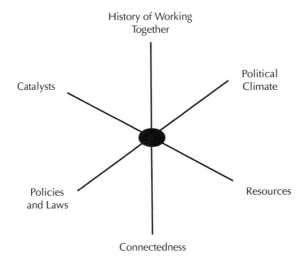

Pause to review the **Spider Web**. The end of each spoke represents a factor. The *center represents the negative impact*, the *outer rim the positive impact* of each factor.

©2002 • EFFECTIVE COLLABORATION

Spider Web, Continued

Third, individually, rate each factor's *current impact* on the collaborative effort by placing a dot on each spoke.

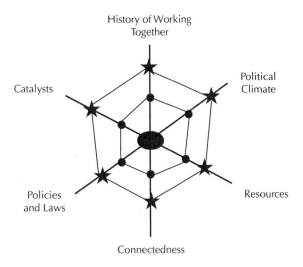

Fourth, use a star to rate the factor for *its realistic impact in three years.*

Fifth, draw a large **Spider Web** for group use. Ask each person to cast their rating.

Finally, recognize where the majority of the *dots* are located. Connect the clusters with a line. This creates the first web – *the current opinions.*

Repeat, connecting the *stars* creating the second web – *the expectation for the future.*

SPIDER WEB, CONTINUED

Use the **Spider Web** to explore the environmental factors impacting your collaborative effort.

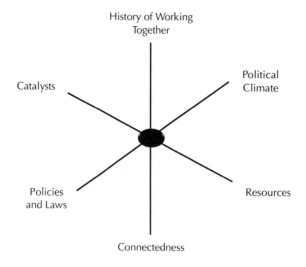

- As a group, our assets include:

  _____

  _____

  _____

  _____

  _____

  _____

- Environmental factors our group can influence include:

  _____

  _____

  _____

  _____

  _____

  _____

6. PROCESSES AND SYSTEMS

Bottom Line Processes

In the process of collaborations creating *new neighborhoods,* the processes involved in communication, decision-making, leading, etc., may shift or require reinvention. The better the fit between the content of change and the people involved, the greater potential for sustainable success.

In developing and using processes complimentary to the collaboration and the people impacted, two key technologies can be used:

- **Community Repository**

    Processes acceptable to the community as a whole.

- **Systems Transaction**

    Processes supporting the internal work of the collaboration.

These two technologies play an important role as collaborative efforts grow. As groups choose to advance their level of collaboration, the effort places greater responsibility on the member organizations and on the community. Most often, these responsibilities are recognized first in the daily processes.

The responsibility is generally recognized in three ways.

1. Is this new way worth the **effort**?
2. How much will this **cost**?
3. Will this jeopardize existing **commitments**?

Answering these questions moves ideas to action, contributes to identifying real and meaningful results, and contributes to building momentum and loyalty. Each of these contributes to sustainable change rather than just conducting an activity.

6. PROCESSES AND SYSTEMS, CONTINUED

The process and system factors address **how** the collaborative effort is conducted. Although equally important, they differ from the community and organizational factors which investigate **what** characteristics define the community and/or organizations.

Regardless of the collaboration linkage, existing processes will be influenced. New opportunities emerge to reengineer these processes.

PROCESS AND SYSTEM FACTORS

Understanding the Community

The habits and traditions of community processes. Knowing that the schools and businesses close during both Christian and Jewish holidays and that the Veterans Day Parade gathers more people community wide than any other event shapes what is important to the community and the processes they use.

Community Development

The processes used to plan and mobilize community issues and strategies. Are hearings common where one group makes decisions or is community wide dialogue routine?

Leadership

The processes for leading change. Is it the expectation of the community that a few people will *lead* and many will follow, or is a high level of participation and engagement evident?

Communication

The formal and informal communication patterns the community relies on to be accurate. What are the common methods of communication and what are the emerging methods?

Research and Evaluation

The processes in place to measure reality with perception. Is this a common process among decision making groups?

Sustainability

The planning, implementation and review processes defining the targeted sustainability. Do people and groups plan for sustainability or hope for it?

PROCESS AND SYSTEM FACTORS, CONTINUED

The Spider Web described in Part 3, Section 5 will be applied with the Process and System Factors.

Begin, building the **Spider Web** by defining common understandings of each factor.

Next, review the **Spider Web**. The end of each spoke represents a factor. The *center represents the negative impact*, the *outer rim the positive impact* of each factor.

Third, individually, rate each factor's *current impact* on the collaborative effort by placing a dot on each spoke.

Fourth, use a star to rate the factor for *its realistic impact in three years*.

Fifth, draw a large **Spider Web** for group use. Ask each person to cast their rating.

Finally, recognize where the majority of the *dots* are located. Connect the clusters with a line. This creates the first web – *the current opinions*.

Repeat, connecting the *stars* creating the second web – *the expectation for the future*.

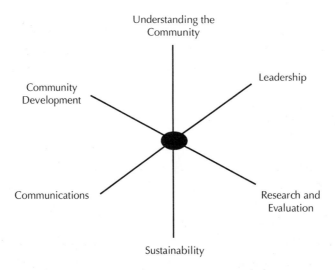

Process and System Factors, Continued

Identify the areas of greatest strengths and weaknesses. Discuss each factor recognizing the gap between the dots and stars. The factor demonstrating the widest gap between the dot and star clusters may identify the area where most work is needed.

_____

_____

_____

_____

_____

_____

_____

_____

_____

_____

_____

_____

_____

_____

_____

_____

_____

_____

_____

_____

_____

_____

_____

REALITY CHECK

Information and application in Part 3 addresses the six technologies important in building and sustaining collaborative efforts. While the work of any collaborative effort will be understood, endorsed and practiced among its members, it is critical to communicate among and with people and organizations who are not directly involved.

This **Reality Check** provides a blueprint to describe a collaborative effort, its intention, membership and actions to and with a broad cross section of people and organizations. It is important to describe the effort in straightforward language, not *agency talk*

The blueprint can serve as the base for developing brochures, Web sites, presentations and other methods of awareness. It also serves as a common communication tool for members.

Blue Print

_____
Name of Collaborative Effort

What is the issue our group is concerned about? and our vision for the future?

_____

_____

_____

_____

_____

What is the role of this collaborative effort? our mission?

_____

_____

_____

_____

_____

Blue Print, Continued

The result the effort is seeking includes:

_____

_____

_____

_____

_____

Initially, the specific actions the groups will take include:

_____

_____

_____

_____

_____

The strengths of our community support this collaborative effort needs include:

_____

_____

_____

_____

_____

Assets the group uses in the process of collaborating include:

_____

_____

_____

_____

_____

_____

PART 4 — PRACTICAL TOOLS

Part 4 provides practical tools and applications of information learned and decisions made in Parts 1, 2 and 3, including:

- **Five Tools to assist with communication and decision making**
- *Trouble Guide*
- **Other resources and references**

Working collaboratively becomes more common place each year. Outcomes or results are popular measures of performance. But, experience and research demonstrates breakthroughs that leap beyond traditional or expected results.

At times, collaborative results make profound history and other times not. No two collaborative efforts are or should be considered the same. Investing in four resources described tailor collaborative efforts for the unique situations facing every group.

1. **Belief** of Stewardship,
2. **Four Core Principles** strengthening capacity, including Community, Capacity, Collaboration and Servant Leadership coupled with,
3. **Four Engagement Factors** mobilizing Core Principles and Stewardship, and
4. **Six Gears or Technologies** framing collaborative operations and infrastructure.

On the outside, working collaboratively may appear to make the usual pace of accomplishment slower. However, when success is examined new habits and traditions of work begin to emerge. Applying the information, tools, techniques and strategies presented in Parts 1, 2 and 3 produce two characteristics, that…

- challenge tradition and,
- elevate accountability with new levels of understanding, trust and competency.

Such intense focus on working collaboratively may appear to cause unmanageable stress. At times leaving people aching for *the old way* of doing things. The real issue is not how many hours are logged, but the steps taken that make a real and positive difference. There are critical decisions to be made at every stage of working collaboratively.

FIVE PRACTICAL TOOLS

Five practical tools have been designed and used with collaborative efforts where...

- **Diverse groups of people** strive to move beyond activities to **positive sustainable systems**.
- These systems **strengthen individual and group capacity** to address problems and/or issues.

1. Circle of Common Ground

The circle of common ground helps define the contributions multiple groups bring to commonly held concerns or interests. It helps reduce conflict and competition while supporting cooperation.

2. Fishbone Profile

The fishbone profile contributes to creating a system of support by defining the desired outcomes and the tasks needed to reach the outcomes. The fishbone contributes to defining specific roles and responsibilities of individuals, groups and organizations.

3. Service Structures

Generally, six types of services may be provided by organizations and collaborative efforts. Using the service structure clarifies the mission of the collaborative effort, and guides prioritization of services that make the best investment in reaching desired outcomes.

4. Support Hubs

Regardless of the identified services to be delivered, a variety of tasks and roles must take place, many simultaneously. The support hub helps groups make decisions about tasks and who will have responsibility to carry out the tasks. Support hubs contribute to clarification among collaborative members.

5. Commitment Profiles

Commitment grows when individual and group needs are met, both personally and professionally. The strength of any collaborative level is elevated when members are responsible for their individual needs. The collaborative effort is enhanced when members contribute and are respectful and sensitive to the needs of other members.

1. CIRCLE OF COMMON GROUND

Process

Each group *owns* a cut of the circle. Each group identifies the resources, beliefs, etc. they have in common with the issue and the other groups. Second, they identify what they can or will share, and third, what they bring that is unique to the collaborative effort.

> Example: Of four Youth Development Groups, they share **common ground** of providing positive youth development services based on the same principles and methods of work. Together, they **share** a large base of volunteers an camping programs, and each provides unique education programs for different ages of youth.

Situation

When diverse groups and people come together to work on common concerns, up to 85% of the problems they face are process in nature.[24] The *Circle of Common Ground* [25] provides a group process that engages understanding and resources each brings to the collaborative effort. Use of the *Circle* reduces competition and increases cooperation, justifies roles and contributes to the reduction of duplications.

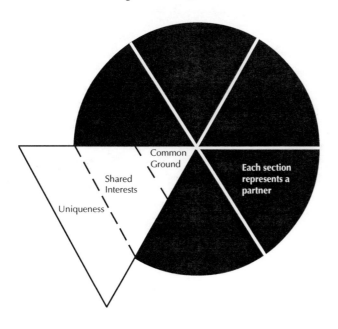

Partner – University Extension Service
Common Ground – Volunteer-based, Faculty Staffed, Focused on youth and families, Non-regulating public organization
Shared Interests – Year around education services, Public funded, Results/outcome based, Committed to sustainability
Uniqueness – Research-based, Non-biased education, Locally based University access

[24]Demming, 1992
[25]Hogue, 1998

2. FISHBONE PROFILE

Process

The fishbone was first introduced in Total Quality Management as a method to outline work:

- **The Head** represents the vision and mission of the collaborative effort.
- **The Spine** describes the principles by which the collaborative effort works.
- **The Upper Bones** represent the outcomes or end results – the very reason for the collaborative effort to exist.
- **The Lower Bones** describe the infrastructure of the collaborative effort. It is common to have bones represent one or more of the identified categories.

Each bone of the fishbone may be used to describe intentions and accomplishments. The fishbone can be effectively used by groups when drawn on large paper where each person has opportunities to contribute their opinions, ideas and thoughts to the profile.

Situation

Mapping a profile of what the collaboration is about, what it does, and what are common questions for the people and groups involved, those who could be involved, and allies to the collaborative effort.

Complex information can be visually displayed by using a fishbone profile.

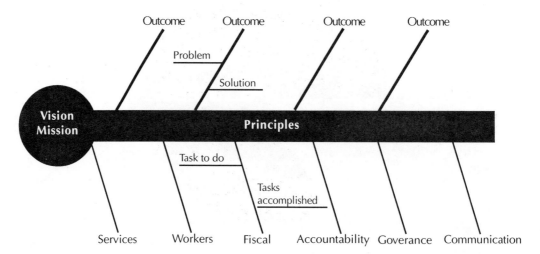

3. Service Structures

Process

As a group, agree on definition of categories.

Next, each partner identifies existing services.

Third, before discussion is help on duplication, gaps, etc., identify desired services – *what is needed to reach the vision.*

Fourth, begin negotiations on where and how services can be provided from the collaborative effort.

Situation

Collaborative efforts, regardless of the linkage, bring together a wide array of services. Merging or realigning to provide a continuum can be complex.

Mapping service structures contributes to strengthening existing, and increasing the capacity of future, services. The six categories parallel the six stages of change.[26]

1. **Awareness**

   General understanding by the community of the service/issue.

2. **Education**

   Education provided on a continued basis for the public, volunteers and/or staff.

3. **One Time Service**

   Providing an event or activity to focus attention to an issue.

4. **Annual Service**

   Implement routine, regular review of service, whether monthly, quarterly or yearly.

5. **Systematic Services**

   Base support services are provided on a regular, and if need be, a daily basis.

6. **Policy Services**

   Policy, practices and procedures provided internally for organization or as public policy.

---

[26]O'Toole, 1995

4. Support Hubs

Process

Hubs may serve as communicators of information, facilitators, mediators or planners. Like the hub of a wheel, they do not control the movement, but serve as a place from which to pivot.

On the practical side, **Hubs** keep members connected by processing and transferring information productively for the members and for the community.

Hubs contribute significantly to maintaining a shared purpose for the members. They serve not only as a communication point for the members, but as the collaboration gains notoriety outside the group, people use **Hubs** as places of contact.

Situation

Collaboration demands innovative work patterns and high levels of servant leadership. Leaders taking risks and offering human, material and social capital through unconventional means become commonplace.

Establish **Hubs**, a collection of people who focus on a specific process of collaboration, enabling members to operative productively.

4. Support Hubs, Continued

Communication Hub

_____

_____

_____

_____

_____

_____

_____

_____

_____

Service Hub

_____

_____

_____

_____

_____

_____

_____

_____

_____

Research & Development Hub

_____

_____

_____

_____

_____

_____

_____

_____

_____

Resource Development Hub

_____

_____

_____

_____

_____

_____

_____

_____

_____

5. COMMITMENT PROFILES

Process

Servant leaders bring *personal and professional* interests to a collaborative effort. Addressing these interests fosters retention and builds commitment.[27]

Begin by asking (and recording) from each person what brings his/her organization to the collaboration.

Second, ask what brings them personally to the understanding individuals' *personal and professional* interests and needs is critical to sustainability.

Third, it is important to know what it will take to keep them as a vital partner. Using these series of questions on *routine* basis build understanding and respect resulting in commitment.

Situation

Regardless of the collaborative linkage, individual and group commitment is a necessary investment in building and sustaining growth. As relationships are established and respect is gained for the *lens* each person brings to the effort, it becomes critical to support commitment.

> "...people desire to be valued, capable, important and understood"[28]

---

[27]Senge, 1998
[28]Victor, 1994

5. Commitment Profiles, Continued

| **Current Interest** | **Keeping Commitment** |
| Participation Includes… | Relays on… |

Personally

_____ _____

_____ _____

_____ _____

_____ _____

_____ _____

_____ _____

_____ _____

_____ _____

_____ _____

Professionally

_____ _____

_____ _____

_____ _____

_____ _____

_____ _____

_____ _____

_____ _____

_____ _____

RESOURCES AND REFERENCES

The following references provide perspectives, strategies, solutions and methods to build sustainable collaborative systems.

Collaboration

Borden, Lynn. Hogue, Teresa. Perkins, Daniel. *Community Collaborations: A Guide to the Standards of Practice Supporting Youth and Families*. NCSREES, United States Department of Agriculture, 1998

Celente, Gerald. *Trends 2000*. New York, New York: Warner Books, 1998

Gray, Barbara. *Collaborating, Finding Common Ground for Multiple Problems*. San Francisco, California: Jossey-Bass, 1989

Hogue, Teresa. *Community Bases Collaboration: Community Wellness Multiplied*. OSU Extension Service, 1993

McRae, Hamish. *The World in 2020: Power, Culture and Prosperity*. Boston, Massachusetts: Harvard Business School Press, 1994

National Network for Collaboration. *Collaboration Framework... Addressing Community Capacity*. Fargo, North Dakota, 1996

National Network for Collaboration. *The Collaboration Framework: The Part We Play in Building Our Community (Video)*. Bend, Oregon: The Chandler Center for Community Leadership, 1998

Webber, John. *Making the Target*. San Francisco, California: Jossey and Bass, 1994

Group Change

Adams, Cindy, et al. *The Change Handbook*. San Francisco, California: Berrett-Koehler Publishers, Inc., 1999

Isaacs, William. *Dialogue and the Art of Thinking Together*. New York, New York: Currency and Doubleday, 1999

Jones, Patricia. Kahaner, Larry. *Say It and Live It*. New York, New York: Currency and Doubleday, 1995

Parker, Glenn M. *Handbook of Best Practices for Teams*. Amherst, Massachusetts: HRD Press, 1996

Stewardship and Leadership

Block, Peter. *Stewardship: Choosing Service over Self-Interest*. San Francisco, California: Berrett-Koehler, 1996

Block, Peter. Blanchard, Ken. Wheatley, Margaret. Autry, James. *Insights on Leadership, Service, Stewardship, Spirit and Servant Leadership*. New York, New York: John Wiley and Sons, Inc., 1996

Stewardship and Leadership, Continue

Covey, S. R. *Principle Centered Leadership*. New York, New York: Summit Books, 1991

Greenleaf, Robert. *The Power of Servant Leadership*. San Francisco, California: Berrett-Koehler Publishers, Inc., 1998

Hesselbein, F. Goldsmith, M. Beckhard, R. *The Leader of the Future*. San Francisco, California: Jossey-Bass, 1996

Jaworski, Joseph. *Synchronicity, The Inner Path of Leadership*. San Francisco, California: Berrett-Koehler Publishers, 1996

Kotter, John P. *Leading Change*. Boston, Massachusetts: Harvard Business School, 1996

Kuczmarski, Thomas D. *Innovation - Leadership Strategies for the Competitive Edge*. Chicago, Illinois: NTC Business Books, 1996

Spears, Larry C. *The Power of Servant-Leadership*. San Francisco, California: Berrett-Koehler Publishers, Inc., 1996

Sustainability and Systems

Loftquist, William. *Discovering the Meaning of Prevention*. Tucson, Arizona: AYD Publications, 1983

Moorthy, P. *Change Methods*. Fast Company, June 1998

Norman, D.A. *The Invisible Computer*. Boston, Massachusetts: MIT Press, 1998

O'Toole, James. *Leading Change*. San Francisco, California: Jossey-Bass Publishers, 1996

Quinn, Robert E. *Deep Change: Discovering the Leader Within*. San Francisco, California: Jossey-Bass, 1996

Senge, Peter M. *The Dance of Change*. New York, New York: Currency-Doubleday, 1999

Senge, Peter M. *The Fifth Discipline*. New York, New York: Currency-Doubleday, 1990

Senge, Peter M. *The Fifth Discipline Fieldbook*. New York, New York: Currency-Doubleday, 1994

Useem, Michael. *The Leadership Moment*. New York, New York: Random House, 1998

Zohar, Danah. *ReWiring the Corporate Brain*. San Francisco, California: Berrett-Koehler Publishers, Inc., 1997

Additional Resources Used in This Book

Demming. *Total Quality Management, A Front View*. Leadership Studies, August 1990

Wilcox, Peter. *Successful Change*. Journal of Leadership, September 1989

COLLABORATION

Virtually every leader today talks about it. Many individuals and groups try to do it. Those **Who** have succeeded understand what *it* is and why it is not just more activity – it is a way of thinking that drives success, from the town hall to the organization boardrooms.

Gaining the edge of success through working collaboratively is no longer an option, it is imperative. As organizations and communities face diminishing resources, complex issues, fast change, and growing populations, new strategic results-oriented actions are needed.

This workbook fosters learning the principles and operations of working together successfully. Through experiential application, the mindset of working collaboratively is strengthened. Embracing different points of views, examining preconceptions coupled with thinking and working together bridges the gap of issues to results. Working together collaboratively is not new, however, it has not been matched recently by productive action.

Results and productive action begin with dialogue. It not only raises the level of shared thinking, it impacts how people act, and in particular, how they act all together. Moving from dialogue to action is commonly expressed in Native American Indian cultures as: *You talk and talk until the talk starts*. This brings together the collective voice from polite competitors to willing collaborators, and collaboration grows into sustainable systems.

The learning, mindset and focus on results framed convenes collaborative work. Sustaining change and strengthening systems of working together is the next step beyond *Effective Collaboration*. As issues become increasingly complex and expectations increase for results, sustainable change requires group, organizations and communities to see how new kinds of insight and collaboration can emerge despite existing deep differences.

Sustainable Change, a new workbook, frames *system patterns* — interconnecting mindsets, results with developing new habits and traditions among and within groups, organizations and communities.

Teresa Hogue, MS

A faculty member of Oregon State University Extension Service and in that capacity serves as the Director of The Chandler Center for Community Leadership. Specializing in increasing community and organization capacity, the Center helps groups, organizations, agencies and businesses increase their ability to address public issues and problems by applying effective leadership, collaborative efforts and policy education. The Center is a public-private collaboration of Oregon State University, Portland State University, Central Oregon Community College, Oregon Corporations and Citizen leaders.

Ms. Hogue has worked extensively in areas of community, youth and family development developing and implementing innovative programs and supporting public policy. She has worked for more than 28 years with both private and public sectors in roles of applying research-based education with diverse groups of people in the United States, Canada, England and the South Pacific.

Among professional organization memberships, Hogue participates in The International Community Development Society, The International Futurist Society, Epsilon Sigma Phi and National Family Resource Coalition. She has been recognized nationally and internationally for her work in bringing together diverse organizations, particularly related to youth and family development.

Teresa Hogue, MS
Director
The Chandler Center for Community Leadership
OSU Extension Service
2600 NW College Way
Bend, Oregon 97701-5998
Phone 541.388.8361
Fax 541.383.8002
teresa.hogue@orst.edu
www.Chandlercenter.com

Jeff Miller, PhD

President and Senior Educator for Innovative Leadership Solutions, a company that believes in the power of individuals to transform themselves, their communities, and their organizations through personal and team learning. He is a member of the educational facilitation team with the Robert K. Greenleaf Center for Servant-Leadership, an associate of the Chandler Center for Community Leadership, and a member of the steering committee for the Medgar Evers Institute.

He has an array of experiences in organizations, change, and human capacity building efforts. His workshops and instruction include topics of collaboration development, staff development, strategic visioning, program design, planning, and evaluation.

He has served as Assistant Director of the North Dakota State University Extension Service with responsibilities for the 4-H Youth Development Program. In this role he served as the administrator responsible for the vision, leadership, and management of the largest volunteer and youth-development organization in North Dakota. For three years, Jeff served as convener for the National Network for Collaboration, a consortium of 20 land-grant universities.

Jeff has worked as a youth and community development specialist for the University of Illinois; evaluation coordinator of a nationally funded human, organizational, and community capacity building initiative; and university extension agent in Georgia.

Miller is a charter member and Vice President of the Association of Leadership Educators. Other professional associations include: the Innovation Network, the American Evaluation Association, and American Society for Training and Development.

Jeffrey P. Miller, Ph.D.
Innovative Leadership Solutions
6526 Oxford Drive
Zionsville, IN 46077
Phone 317.733.8635
Fax 317.733.8636
jeff@inleadsol.com
www.inleadsol.com